Controlling Your Power With N of 1

Turning Your Pain Into Power

By Monchelle Hicks-Whitaker

Monchelle Hicks-Whitaker
Paradisehempfarms@gmail.com

Power

Britannica Dictionary definition of POWER[1]

1: the ability or right to control people or things

2: political control of a country or area

3a: a person or organization that has a lot of control and influence over other people or organizations

3b: a country that has a lot of influence and military strength

4a: *physical force or strength*

4b: military force

4c: *the energy or force that someone or something can produce for movement, work, etc.*

5a: *an ability to do something*

5b: the ability to influence or affect people or things

---

[1] Power Definition & Meaning | Britannica Dictionary

6a: *the right to do something*

6b: *legal or official authority to do something*

7a: energy that can be collected and used to operate machines

7**b:** the electricity that people use

8a: the number of times that a number is to be multiplied by itself

8**b:** a number that results from multiplying a number by itself

9: the ability of an optical device (such as a telescope) to make objects look bigger

Control

Oxford Languages[2]

1. the power to influence or direct people's behavior or the course of events

2. the ability to manage a machine, vehicle, or other moving object

3. *the restriction of an activity, tendency, or phenomenon*

4. *the power to restrain something, especially one's own emotions or actions*

5. *a means of limiting or regulating something*

6. a switch or other device by which a machine is regulated

7. the place where a particular item is verified

---

[2] define CONTROL - Search (bing.com)

8. the base from which a system or activity is directed

9. short for "control key".

10. a group or individual used as a standard of comparison for checking the results of a survey or experiment

11. a member of an intelligence organization who personally directs the activities of a spy

12. a high card that will prevent the opponents from establishing a particular suit

13. *determine the behavior or supervise the running of*

14. *maintain influence or authority over*

15. limit the level, intensity, or number of

16. *remain calm and reasonable despite*

provocation

17. take into account (an extraneous factor that

might affect results) when performing an

experiment

Bullying personalities, rooted in mental
disorders, perpetuate humanity's darkest
evils – from wars to environmental
degradation – but Nature's evolutionary
imperative will ultimately transform human
consciousness, ushering in a golden age of
peace, harmony, and global well-being.

-Monchelle Hicks

INTRODUCTION

One day, as I was watching self-help videos on youtube, going through my usual cycle of entrepreneurial "where to start" type videos, "get your mind right first" type of videos, "self love" videos, and "understanding the mind" type of videos, one of my favorite channels I found while I was in my last relationship on narcissism and narcissistic abuse came on. I really loved that channel because the host is not only a licensed psychologist that specializes in narcissism but she also examines her own experiences along with case studies, other doctor's work and the thousands of clients she has worked with personally and she delivers the information in a way that lets you know she gets it. She isn't just reading from a clinical textbook, she actually understands and wants her viewers to really get it too. So while she uses her expanded vocabulary she is in no way talking over anyone's head or just using a bunch of words to make herself sound smart like some people do that I have experienced.

This particular day one of her videos came in my parade of informational videos I was watching to learn what I needed to do to change my life. In her video she said people with narcissistic personality can change but it's not likely that they

will and she explained that it's because of their

deep insecurity and shame surrounding being

vulnerable. So they can't or won't let their guards

down to receive the help to change. I thought a

person who is narcissistic was just born that way.

Like how a psychopathic person is born without

the ability for empathy. But she said it's

something that develops in non psychopathic

people. I thought "wow, so if it's created, then it

can be destroyed. And if it can be created, it can

be prevented." This curiosity started my journey

of exploring human behavior and evolution.

I began reflecting on my own family and different types of toxic personalities and the effects they cause to a family. Where would we be and what would we have become if we didn't have toxic people and events in our family? Look, my line of thinking is that it all starts with the individual person and every individual comes from a family. You take you wherever you go. If you have a kind and empathetic personality, you are that way in your family and in your community. If you have an antagonistic personality, you are that way with family and non-family even if you strategically choose who to be your true self with. So when I consider my children's

future and them having a better life and becoming better

people for the world, I wonder about what kind of world

they would live in. Other people are dealing with family,

neighbors, coworkers and bosses who have toxic,

antagonistic personalities. I learned this more as I

studied narcissistic abuse. I realized that not only does

my ex have a narcissistic personality but so does my

mom, sister, and a few people that I had welcomed into

my life over the course of my life. As I focused on my

recovery from these relationships, I came to the

realization that antagonism and antagonistic personalities

are founded in manipulation. The manipulation and

deception is so deep that it shapes your subconscious mind, dictates your actions, and negatively affects your health. As I type this I hear a quote from Ida B Wells Barnett, "eternal vigilance is the price of liberation." The Oxford dictionary defines vigilance as the action or state of keeping careful watch for possible danger or difficulties. This is perfect because the manipulation is dangerous and affects your mind. Your mind is how you experience the world. It is your ultimate power. So what we are really talking about is a gross manipulation of your personal power. Sister Ida's statement from her autobiography is so very deep and powerful. Will is not free. The cost of it is your mind. If we are to be liberated from our own harmful toxic traits and patterns and from

the toxic personalities of others, it requires constant

action and counter actions. Eternal vigilance. Intentional

watchful mindfulness and watching with the intent to

reverse or prevent the negative effects. My intention for

this book is to be a guide for people to take back their

power and transform the pains caused by handing over

their power. One thing I have learned (and continue to

learn) is that though this is a constant push-pull battle

with internal self and external self, taking back your

power and buying back your will doesn't have to be an

added toxic stressor. With this book, I want to give you

hope. I want to give you confidence. I want to infuse in

your mind that you can take control of your mental programming that is out of your control. And you can teach it to the next generation both directly through corrections and life lessons and indirectly through observation of your actions. By breaking generational curses you are changing generational patterns. You change biology and gene expression as you change your mind, habits and patterns. To do this you must become aware of them. Not just your own actions but your response to your environment. This covers literally every aspect of your life. It will even affect national leadership we choose, policies put in place, businesses we start and those we support, and even how advertisement is curated. There must be a total change in national and

global social structures. And it all starts with the

individual; you reading this book. In this book I put

together the research, discoveries and thoughts of

experts and thought leaders around the world over time

along with my own experiences. I grew up in the

christian religion and studied different religions

throughout my life so you will find a lot of christian

references. However I try to keep it balanced with

respect to other people's beliefs and spirituality, though I

personally hold no religious beliefs now. I want to break

past the religious language barriers and get to a deeper

understanding of ourselves and individual people and a

collective humanity and how we affect each other and how our environment affects us. What I know is that once this understanding is had in you, you will be able to examine yourself and learn where the issues lie and how to reverse engineer it and reprogram yourself. The result is better relationships, improved health, and a more empathetic human society. And as this evolution takes place with great intentionality, we will move closer and closer to a type one global civilization that is truly civilized and not warful, antagonistic, greedy, and power hungry. You are the best knower of you. As you read this book, be honest with yourself. This is a very personal process but you are not alone in it. Start where you see fit in your life and make small changes. Create new patterns. Remain mindful and allow yourself to become more empathetic of others, kind to yourself, and confident in your ability to control your own powers over your will. You deserve to live out your programming. Liberation is your birthright. The only way to truly be liberated is to control your programming. Your programming dictates your will. There is no such thing as free will. The cost is your mental, biological, and social programming.

Chapter One

Taking Back Your Power

TAKE BACK CONTROL OF YOUR POWER/ TAKE

BACK CONTROL OF YOURSELF

YOUR SELF IS YOUR POWER.

POWER = SELF

Self Control = power to control yourself.

Self Love = power to love yourself

Self Study = power to study yourself

Ect., ect., ect.

Your power is yourself. It is who you are. Self-control is important because if you don't control yourself and you lose control or control of yourself, you lose control of your power. Now someone else can come in and take control of your power or yourself. Some ways we lose control and relinquish control of our power are through marketing ads, healthcare, social influence, and belief systems.

Control the Power of Your Mind/ Mind Control

The key to marketing is mind control[3,4,5]. Your mind is a part of the whole of yourself. Your mind is a piece of

---

[3] 7 Psychology Tricks to Get Inside Your Customers' Heads - AllBusiness.com
[4] 46 Psychological Marketing Examples for Smarter Marketing (crobox.com)
[5] 14 Psychological Marketing Tips for Customer Mind Control (disruptiveadvertising.com)

you; a part of self. Remember, self is power. Your mind

is a part of your power. Hypnosis has been experimented

with by people dating back to the third century B.C.E..[6]

Thought to be an effective form of mind control for

many purposes including healing and national defense.[7]

One technique used in hypnotic mind control is

repetition. First, the person has to be in a relaxed and

trusting state.[8] With marketing and advertising, people

reading, watching, and listening receive messages on

repeat, often attached to pleasing and attractive sensory

stimuli such as catchy songs, yummy scents, or funny

short skits. Guards are down and the message is received

over and over until one's perception is altered[9]. You

---

[6] Ancient Hypnosis - Hypnosis in History
[7] MK-Ultra (history.com)
[8] How Hypnotherapy Works - The Process in Four Steps (hypnosis.edu)
[9] Make Them Buy: Hypnosis in Advertising (instituteofclinicalhypnosis.com)

weren't thinking about food until you saw that Lil Ceasar's commercial playing for the third time between your favorite show or the Domino's pizza or Taco Bell ad playing during the radio or Spotify music break. You smell the fries cooking outside McDonald's or the chicken frying from outside KFC while you pass by on your way home from work. Now you have a taste for pizza, chicken, or a burger when you weren't even hungry for real. You know you have that food in the fridge marinating but you got a strong urge to stop real quick to pick up a "snack". Or you tell yourself "I don't feel like cooking anyway." Plans changed because the mind-control marketing techniques worked on you subconsciously and you were unaware that you needed to take control of your power. The same thing happened during the COVID-19 pandemic with face masks.[10]

Doctors were reporting both the effectiveness and the

ineffectiveness of wearing face masks[11]. The message on

the effects of not wearing masks was on the CDC

website[12], on the entrance to every public serving

company, playing on news outlets and tv ads over and

over.[13,14] "Wearing face masks reduces the spread of the

coronavirus that leads to COVID-19 infection.", "Must

wear a mask.", "No mask. No service." Pictures of

masks posted all over the country. Mask-wearing became

a rule in this country and throughout the world. At one

time in what feels like the distant past, no one could go

---

[10] Timeline: CDC mask guidelines during the COVID pandemic - Los Angeles Times (latimes.com)
[11] FAUCI SAYS NO MASKS (youtube.com)
[12] Timeline: CDC mask guidelines during the COVID pandemic - Los Angeles Times (latimes.com)
[13]We Have a Cheap, Effective Way to Limit COVID-19 Spread | TIME
[14] Why scientists say wearing masks shouldn't be controversial (sciencenews.org)

into a store with a face mask on[15]. During the pandemic, no one could go in the store without one or they faced being attacked by other people[16,17,18,19]. Yes, citizens were attacking other citizens for not wearing face masks and shamed and ostracized for choosing not to vaccinate[20,21,22]. This was despite medical and scientific research and peer-reviewed studies done by many doctors and medical professionals including an alliance of clinic owners and more than 16 doctors called the "Front Line COVID-19 Critical Care Alliance" that was

---

[15] No Hoodies Allowed in Harlem Businesses, Signs Warn - Central Harlem - New York - DNAinfo

[16] 'Incomprehensible': Confrontations over masks erupt amid COVID-19 crisis - ABC News (go.com)

[17] Face masks don't restrict oxygen or contribute to carbon dioxide buildup: study | Fox News

[18] Man hit in head during mask confrontation (youtube.com)

[19] Man attacked police when stopped for not wearing face mask, NSW court hears | 7NEWS (youtube.com)

[20] Utah woman assaulted by fellow Walmart shopper for not wearing mask, police say (youtube.com)

[21] Man stabbed, others assaulted during dueling vaccine protest in LA (youtube.com)

[22] Fight breaks out on plane over face masks (youtube.com)

co-founded by Dr. Pierre Kory, the doctor who testified

before congress in December 2020 and Dr. John

Campbell, a retired emergency room nurse and PhD

doctor in England who became popular on youtube for

teaching about COVID-19, how it spreads, what it does

in the body and research on treatments including

peer-reviewed Ivermectin studies and protocols on

dosage and use in COVID-19 treatment and prevention,

and messages from the surgeon general stating that

masks worn by the public are not effective at stopping

the spread of the coronavirus that leads to

COVID-19.[23,24,25] People chose to allow their emotions

to be led by the media and gave up control of their power

---

[23] The importance of wearing masks in curtailing the
COVID-19 pandemic - PMC (nih.gov)
[24] U.S. Surgeon General: face masks are not effective in
preventing spread of COVID-19 (kcrg.com)
[25] Fauci Said Masks 'Not Really Effective in Keeping Out
Virus,' Email Reveals (newsweek.com)

to examine the scientific research that shows that face masks neither prevented the spread of coronavirus nor significantly lowered the viral load in the air. Videos went viral on social media of people acting out of control; actually physically assaulting other people who chose not to wear a mask, when if those hysterically violent and fearful people would have, instead of violently attempting to control others, taking control of their own self (power) and using their power (self) to dig deeper into the scientific data on the effectiveness of face masks to stop the spread of covid, they wouldn't be forever on film looking and acting crazy. You have the power to control yourself. When you hand over that power to a professional to control, you no longer have the power to make the best right choices for yourself. You then become subject to unethical practices and actions. You then open yourself to being enslaved, roped, dragged around, and hung by your own uncontrolled emotions and irrational thoughts and actions.

Control the Power of Your Body/ Body Control

Doctors, Nutritionists, Pharmacists, Psychiatrists, etc. Study particular fields of health science. They invest tons of hours (years worth) into their craft. They know their fields of study but they do not know you. You are the best possible knower of self. When you give them total control of your body, you give them control of your power because your body is a part of your total self which is your power. When they are in control of their own power, they control the powers of their mind and knowledge. If they are acting in their own higher power (self) by listening to their patients, practicing patient-centered care, not rushing to meet a quota, and living up to their Hippocratic Oath, they use the control of their power to share with you.[26] In sharing with you, they meet you with your power. When you take control of your power, you have observed yourself and you meet them with their power. This is sharing or exchanging information, which is a meeting of the powers of your minds.[27,28] You control your own power by doing your own study of self (N of 1) using the power of your mind and brain to analyze data and information and making the best choice for yourself without leaving the power of choice to the doctor to control what happens to your body.[29] When we do this we dramatically decrease the

---

[26] 6 Things Doctors Do to Frustrate Patients - ABC News (go.com)
[27] Patient-centred care explained - Better Health Channel
[28] Why Is Patient-Centered Care Important? (usfhealthonline.com)
[29] Self-Advocacy: Know Your Rights as a Patient (webmd.com)

number of disorders caused by medicine and deaths

caused by physicians.[30] Think about it, 12 million adults

are misdiagnosed annually in the United States[31]

resulting in 40,000 to 80,000 deaths each year. And

women and minorities are 20-30% more likely to be

misdiagnosed[32].

Control the Power of your Spirit/Spirit Control

Your choice and your will are your ultimate powers.

Your power to choose is directly related to your ability to

decide for yourself. It is your freedom. Exercising that

power is your spirit or your energy. This will of spirit is

the energy that powers every living thing. The freedom

---

[30] Johns Hopkins Medicine Researchers Identify Health Conditions Likely to be Misdiagnosed | Johns Hopkins Medicine

[31] Twelve million patients misdiagnosed yearly in America, says VA researcher

[32] Why Getting Medically Misdiagnosed Is More Common Than You May Think (healthline.com)

to exercise our will is a natural right of humans. You lose control of these powers when you accept the lie that there is someone or some knowledge base outside of yourself that knows you better than you can know yourself. Self-doubting your own powers leads to losing your will and handing over your choice which is your power. It negatively affects every part of your life and being. Ever hear the saying "faint of heart" or "faint of spirit"? When you lose your power to control your will/spirit and self-doubt kicks in, confidence is lost, making way for fear. Faint of Heart is fearfulness due to low spirit or will. By taking control of your spirit you make choices for yourself. You hold yourself accountable for those choices, motivating and empowering yourself to study more deeply yourself and your place in humanity and the world around you. You become more confident in your powers and your abilities to exercise your freedom of will. Your will is not free. It is paid with the energy you pour into yourself and losing it comes at the cost of giving up control of your power.

YOU ARE SO POWERFUL!

When is someone said to be powerful? I'm talking about everyday people. When you tell someone they are powerful, what are you talking about??? What do you mean by "powerful"? They are strong. They are capable of great things. They have shown you the ability to control their actions. They are in control of self or an aspect of themselves. Think about it. Your friend is always there for others, warm, loving, and selfless. They have been through some tough times. Is frustrated because of a situation at work. And they still show up for their loved ones. When yal hang out and vent about your lives, they still make space to be there for you like you're there for them. That friend is POWERFUL. That friendship is POWERFUL! It takes power and self-control to not allow the negativity of the world to change you, but instead continue to show up for others and pour love into the world.

The Power To Attract

You are magnetic. What is attracted to you and what you are attracted to is relative to your energetic focus. Your energetic focus is determined by your subconscious thoughts. Now to explain a little deeper, your attraction or ability to attract is compared to a magnet simply because it attracts. Not in the same way that a magnet attracts. Magnets attract the opposite at their poles. The north pole attracts the south pole and the south pole attracts the north pole. Negative attracts positive and positive attracts negative. This is not how your mind works. We don't attract the opposite of our thoughts. We attract what we think about. Now the ends of the magnet have the strongest attraction and the center of the magnet has the weakest attraction. Our minds are like that in a sense. Our most polarized thoughts have the strongest attraction, whether negative or positive. The average person has between 70,000 and 80,000 thoughts per day. All kinds of thoughts. Not every thought is magnetic. Some thoughts are like the middle of the magnet. It's the thoughts we think about the most, the thoughts with the most focused attention, and the thoughts we focus on with the strongest emotional ties that we attract to us and that creates our reality.   Make those thoughts

ones that align with your actions towards your vision for

your best life.

NOTES:

Chapter Two

Love/Romance/Connections

After trust is abused, not trusting is a natural response

for self-preservation. It is a symptom of relinquishing

that power and not getting a good return.

I have felt, and in many ways still feel, that it is very wise advice to "trust no one". While one must protect self, it is painful to have no one to trust. It is human nature to connect with other human beings; to form bonds. And without a level of trust, there is no real bond or connection. I had to go back in my mind and identify the cause of mistrust for other humans. I discovered that while there were definite situations and events in early childhood that shook my sense of trust, there is no isolated event that led me here. "Trust no one." Rather a sequence of events. A lifetime of patterns. As a rebellion against my fear of being vulnerable, I would take a person how they presented, ignoring the obvious red flags, not realizing that not everyone is deserving of my vulnerability. When the rose-colored glasses came off and the truth was seen, it left me feeling betrayed, foolish, violated, and lied to, making it even more difficult to trust. To not trust became easier, and less painful. It made me want to not desire to trust. It became easier to refocus my attention and distract myself so I didn't have to face the moment of choice. To trust or not to trust. Some parts of you you don't even notice exist until it's in pain. I started to become aware of that moment in a relationship when I had to decide if I'm going to let go and trust the person or keep my guard up and not trust. I began to realize there is power in choosing to hold up that guard and not trust. Not to let anyone into the most vulnerable parts of myself. I can't shake the need for connection on such an intimate level though. The need is still there. I can't bury it in distractions. Ever so often it climbs up from underground like a Casada and if I am not careful with where I place my trust, it dies again shortly after mating, just like casadas do. Then I bury it again somewhere during the mourning process. This is a vicious cycle and if I am honest, the real abuser and killer of my trust is myself. My poor choices. My unhealed mental and emotional state. My being too eager for connection. So anxious that I choose to believe whatever lies I was presented with. Ignoring my intuition and only seeing the mask of my desires instead of the truth of the individual situation. The truth is and has always been somewhere between blind faith and guarded mistrust. To see it for what it is and accept it as it is, not how I wish it to be. Not how they present it to be, but exactly how it is. There is even greater power in that. Truth. To live in and enjoy the moment with eyes wide open in full acceptance of reality, not compromising boundaries but being attentive to my emotions and aware of my intuition.

I have only gotten there in theory; Not yet in practice. So for now it's "to be continued" on this… I'll let you know how it goes .

NOTES:

Chapter 3

Temptation and Enlightenment

I was often shooting in the dark, but God came to shine

light into my darkness. Then I was able to see my target

.

The darkness is often viewed as evil or something bad. It's associated with the devil, bad or wrong actions, a scary place, a black hole that rips everything apart. What if I tell you that the dark isn't bad at all? What if I tell you that darkness is filled with good things?

Out Of Darkness

There were many dark ages in human history. The Dark Ages are periods in time when a group of people lacked certain information needed for their evolution. The Illuminati or the Enlightened Ones were a group of people with specific information.

Side note:

il - lum - i - nati - on

The - light - self - people - collective

Nati - on

People - collective

Take a black hole, for example. What goes into a black
hole is ripped apart. Separated down to its smallest
sub-particles. The black hole is so dark that it can not be
seen. It's just darkness and what goes in, once at the
outermost grip on it, the event horizon, can not escape.
Not even light particles can escape the event horizon.
That's why it's called a black hole. At the same time,
particles shoot out of the darkness. It comes out as light
called Hawking radiation. From that Hawking radiation,
new things are formed. Even in the darkness, there is
light. The particles are energy and information.
Information is carried by and on the light. Sight happens
because light enters the eye. Light containing
information. The amount of light determines how much
can be seen.

Dark Ages ~ periods in time when the masses of people

lack information or light.

"Shine light on the topic" ~ to give information on a

subject matter.

Recently, people have been talking more about shadow

work and light work. What is that?

Shadow work is a term coined by Swiss psychoanalyst

and inventor of analytical psychology, Carl Jung. Jung

believed that everyone has traits they keep hidden from

their conscious awareness because it is too undesirable to

confront. These are traits such as trauma or resentment.

He believed that the shadow self is expressed by

pointing out these flaws in another person. Jung believed

that by confronting these hidden traits and accepting

them, we bring it to our conscious awareness and merge it with the psyche, creating a whole healed self. Light work, just like shadow work, is hidden from our psyche. Except light work is the hidden good parts of yourself and by confronting the light self, we become more creative.[33,34,35]

From my understanding of what Carl Jung was saying about shadow work, when we face our innermost self, we will discover the things that are too painful for us to look at. That doesn't mean that deep down we are the things that trigger us. But it means that we have unresolved traumas as a result of that thing that we see in someone else and it reminds us of the traumatic event or

---

[33] What Is Shadow Work And How Do You Start Practicing It? (harpersbazaar.com)
[34] innershadowwork.com
[35] What are examples of shadow work? - Processing Therapy

of the person that we resent. Doing the work of sitting

with yourself and facing and examining that part of your

psyche will shed light on what was hidden within and

bring acceptance of that experience to the surface of your

consciousness. So now you can discover tools to help

you cope with or release the pain of the experience. And

in doing so, bring less pain to yourself and others. Now

if the pain is associated with a sex trauma or narcissistic

abuse, for example, and the trigger is cause by seeing or

experiencing those same traits, characteristics, or actions

in another person, that does not mean that you are hiding

some hidden desires for narcissism or sexual deviance

in your subconscious mind like some people misinterpret

shadow work and shadow self to mean. It just means

you've hidden the memories of those events to protect

your mind. It is a perfectly normal trauma response. A part of your healing journey may look like you raising awareness to narcissistic abuse, sexual molestation, rape, domestic violence, bullying or any other trauma you've experienced that is behind the triggers. Owning your experiences is powerful and standing in your truth despite what other people say is healing and a result of doing your shadow work.

"Shadow self", "Light self", dark places, and darkness are all referring to self. And not necessarily the bad or negative parts of yourself, but just the parts of self where little of no light has been shown. Parts of yourself that you don't know about or haven't examined to get information on. It all starts with your mind. Consciousness. Awareness. Once you sit with yourself, doing self study or N of 1, you examine yourself, which is shining light on parts of yourself, your thoughts, emotions, actions, physical body, character,... your self, to get information, knowledge and understanding about yourself. What you discover can be positive or negative. It can also be relatively good or bad.

Side note: when a doctor or scientist examines a subject matter, they use special lights.

It is important to note that positive is relatively good or bad depending on the situation (quality, quantity and location) and the same goes for negative.

Adam and Eve

There is a certain confidence that comes with knowledge or light. When you know that you know something, you have confidence in that area. You are proud to have knowledge of it or proud to stand in that light or knowing. When it is something you don't know or are in the dark about, you aren't confident in those areas. Now imagine a time when there was something about you that you didn't know but someone else knew. That moment when you came into the awareness that someone else knew something about you that you hadn't discovered yet about yourself is a vulnerable moment. You feel naked or exposed. You may even feel ashamed. Adam and Eve tried to hide their shame by covering up their nakedness.[36]

---

[36] The Holy Bible Genesis 3:7,10

The Tree Of Knowledge Of Good And Evil

"For you will know the tree by its own fruit..." Luke 6:44. The fruit of the tree of knowledge of good and evil[37] is much like an apple tree or tree of apples. The fruit on the tree is the apples. The fruit on the tree in the garden is the knowledge of good and evil. In Luke 6:44, the author uses imagery to talk about the actions of humans. The tree is a human and the fruit is what the human produces. To eat is to consume, ingest or take in. When Adam and Eve *ate* the *fruit* of the *tree*, they consumed or *took in* light or *knowledge* about *themselves* (or humanity), specifically what can be viewed as good or evil about the world. This new knowledge caused them to look at themselves and notice some things about themselves. It was presented first to Eve by the serpent.

[37] The Holy Bible Genesis 2:9

The light was shown on her or to her by the serpent. Basically he told her about herself and she bit. She ate the "apple". She consumed that information or took in that light. She was so amazed by it that she turned to Adam to share it with him. Now in Genesis 3:6 KJV says "...she took of the fruit thereof, and did eat, and gave also unto *her husband with her*: and he did eat". This means Adam was right there with her when the serpent was talking to his wife, Eve. After listening to the serpent, Eve saw that the fruit was good for food, looked good and good for wisdom and decided to eat the fruit and shared it with Adam, her husband, who was there with her. She consumed the knowledge first but Adam was right there with her and he chose to consume it also. Then both their eyes were opened in verse 7. They knew

they were naked. Meaning they were bare or vulnerable.
When you start to do your self study and begin to open
your eyes to the truth about who you are, it can put you
in a vulnerable state. To be naked is to be raw or bare. In
order to truly study yourself, you have to be honest with
yourself. Wearing no stories or excuses. Bare,
transparent truth. Some things you learn about yourself
will cause you shame. In verse 7 of Genesis chapter 3,
Adam and Eve saw that they were naked and sewed fig
leaves together and made themselves aprons. What does
that mean? They used the fig leaves as a covering. What
is a covering? Protection. It says they sewed them
together and made an apron. The thread they used to sew
together their covering is the lies and excuses we tell
ourselves and others to protect our ego and cover up the

shameful truths about ourselves. But they didn't sow together complete coverings. They sewed together aprons, which only covers the front. This reminds me of an old saying "you can't save your face and your ass at the same time." This means you have to decide if you will lie about your life and get in trouble. They chose to cover their front. Meaning they chose to create stories to hide the shame of their naked truth. When they heard God walking, they hid themselves amongst the trees of the garden. See, they had already been consuming the fruit of the other trees in the garden. So they already had that knowledge. Sometimes we hide behind our background knowledge. We hide behind other sources of truths to distract from the truth of our shame and vulnerability. So they tried to hide and keep secret their shame they just discovered about themselves by sewing and putting together stories of lies they wore like aprons and still hid from the presence of God. but God is Truth. They couldn't hide. They had to come out from behind the trees. But the bible never says they took off the covering they made. Even after God called them out, they started speaking their lies. Maybe that's why the bible says they sewed aprons instead of coverings that covered their whole body like a cloak and dress. In verse 10, Adam started speaking and telling on himself. But God not only heard what they said, He also saw the truth that Adam and Eve didn't say. God knew exactly what would happen when they ate the fruit. See, when knowledge is given too soon or in the wrong context, the shock and shame can cause undesired effects from depression, anxiety and suicide to abuse of alcohol, drugs and other vices to anger, rage and murder. This is why it's important for you to do your own n of 1 and be prepared mentally, emotionally and physically for what you might uncover about yourself. They stood before God (TRUTH) wearing their aprons (LIES)... bad lies at that LOL. God knew what would happen if they ate from the tree before they were ready. He asked just two questions, Genesis 3:11 "...Who told thee that thou wast naked? Hast thou eaten of the tree, whereof I commanded thee that thou shouldest not eat?" Who told you that you're naked? And Did you eat from that tree I told you not to eat from? And straight away they began to lie and place blame. Adam blamed God for giving him the woman and the woman for giving him the fruit that he ate. He didn't answer the question directly nor did he take accountability for his actions. Remember, Eve didn't go search out Adam and feed him unknown fruit. He was right there with her when she took and ate the fruit and shared it with him. At no point does the bible say that Adam spoke against what the serpent was saying nor does it say that he rejected the fruit. And Eve also placed blame. When God asked her what she had done she failed to take accountability for her actions, blaming the serpent for being charming. As you spend time with yourself in meditation and self study, memories will begin to surface that you must face and confront. You will be tempted to place blame and make up stories and excuses for yourself. What I had to realize and what I want to let you know is that you are confronting yourself. This is your own self study. It serves you no

good to lie to yourself. Freedom comes when you are

honest with yourself. For me, when I began to examine

my relationships with my children and study the aspect

of myself that is motherhood, I blamed my childhood,

society, the person I was in a long term toxic relationship

with. And there is truth in those stories I was telling

myself (or the trees in the garden I was hiding behind).

But the vulnerable, shameful, honest truth that I was

avoiding is that I made every choice that I made. No one

made me do it. I chose to have children young. I chose to

not go to counseling even though I knew my childhood

screwed me up. I chose to get in that relationship with

someone I didn't know enough about and then I chose to

move him into my home. I chose to engage in every

argument and to stay in that relationship until I chose to walk away. I chose to stay in those negative emotions that were produced in those situations. Even when I decided to start my own business and rebuild my relationships with my children, all of my choices were made from those negative places. I chose to push forward without properly healing. The raw truth is that all of my choices are what created my current life at that time. And if I was to change my life and change my choices, I absolutely had to confront this truth and accept it for what it is so that I could let it go and begin to heal. You can push forward and do some great things without healing if you push hard enough. But you will be dead inside. You will have to work even harder later just to keep producing while constantly maintaining the lies you tell yourself and others in order to hide your shame. If you take the time you deserve now, no matter where you are in life, to examine yourself in transparent, honest vulnerability, it will be easier for you, going forward, to tend to the garden of your mind. The choices you make will reflect your healing and growth and you will be able to produce with ease instead of though blood sweat and tears like Adam and Eve[38]

---

[38] Genesis 3

NOTES:

Chapter 4

Perception is Everything

Perception is the process by which individuals interpret and organize sensory information from the environment to produce a meaningful experience of the world. It involves the recognition, interpretation, and conscious experience of sensory stimuli, such as sights, sounds, smells, tastes, and touch. Perception is influenced by various factors, including past experiences, expectations, cultural background, and individual differences. It is a fundamental cognitive function that allows humans and other organisms to navigate and respond to their surroundings effectively.

Our perception is how we see the world. Exactly what we perceive and how we perceive it is created and shaped by a few factors. Some include your biology, diet, mental & emotional states, experience, and environment. Each of these are intertwined and work together to influence our sensory perception and reasoning. It is important to understand how you think, perceive and view the world and why. It is important to know this and take this into account when doing your N of 1 studies. Having an inaccurate or unproductive view of yourself, other people, or the world around you can lead to delayed healing, lack of self trust and self confidence, poor quality of relationships, a limit of healthy relationships, an abundance of unhealthy relationships, and dreams deferred and unattained, or unenjoyed and under-appreciated. It can even lead to poor physical health. The question is, "how does one come to and maintain a healthy and balanced perception?"

The mind and sensory perception

There are more than thirty areas in the brain, totalling about 50% of the brain, that are responsible for sight. When it comes to interpreting what you see, there is the awareness of the thing. Awareness does not require physical sight. It's a knowing that a thing is in your presence. Then there is the decoding of what the thing is. We call it labels or names or classifications. Then there is the identification of its purpose or the reasoning as to why it is. The awareness that it is, the understanding what it is and the identifying why it is are processes that take place in three different parts of our brain. They work together (along with other senses) to form our perception of the thing. If there is any alteration to just one of these processes or just one part of one of these processes, our entire perception of the thing is changed. Smells attached to events can create an emotion in our minds that locks in the memory for what seems like forever. What the smell means to you can change your perception of the memory of the event. The taste of the meal at a wedding can affect the perception of the event. Your senses play a large part in your perception. Your senses take place in your mind and your mind is run on chemical processes. Those chemical processes can be affected and altered by what you eat, environmental factors, and situations or events that require extreme emotional energy. When a smell is associated with a traumatic event, it can be passed down to offspring. Smells and tastes develop in the womb. Whether or not you like a smell is defined based on your previous experience with the scent. Even generational and cultural experiences influence your perception of smell. In studies, mice that were given electric shock then sprayed with almonds developed a receptor for the almond scent and a dislike for the scent. Their offspring who were never introduced to the almond/shock disliked the almond scent. Whereas the mice whose parents never experienced the almond/shock and they also never received it, did not have a negative response to the almond scent. How sensing works, input comes in through the receptors to your brain (called bottoms up perception) or your brain tells you if you like it or not based on other sensations that alter your perception (called top down perception). For example, if you try your favorite food made by a new cook that looks good, the flavor is more likely to be pleasing to you because of other sensory information besides the taste like the sight and memory of the food. Your mind has specific receptors to match neurotransmitters. If that taste or olfactory receptor isn't prescient, you can't smell or taste the scent or flavor. Your senses work together with memory, emotions, and genetics to create perception.

What you eat

Your food breaks down to chemicals called nutrients. The nutrients break down to micronutrients that either create neurotransmitters that send action commands to your brain and body, or they act as neurotransmitters or they tell neurotransmitters what to do. Meaning they play significant roles in how your brain and body functions and experiences itself and the world it's in. perception. Beta Carotene is a micronutrient in fruits, veggies and grains that gives it its yellow, red and orange color. Consuming large amounts of beta carotene helps maintain healthier hearing. Omega 3 fatty acid is a nutrient that can protect your eyes against degeneration. Magnesium is a micronutrient that helps fight depression and also lowers stress when combined with Vitamin B6.

Environmental factors

Toxins in the environment like pesticides, herbicides, and micro plastics can stick to your cells, cause DNA lesions and increase oxidative stress leading to diseases like tumors and cancer, Alzheimers, heart failure, respiratory problems and other diseases and disorders.

Events of extreme emotions

When something happens that you perceive as good, pleasing and exciting, hormones are released in your brain. Those hormones are attached to memories and saved to storage in your brain. Those hormones stimulate hormones in the body and set off a chain of events that reduces oxidative stress. And likewise, when a traumatic event happens, your brain produces hormones that attach to memories that are stored. Those hormones stimulate hormones produced in the body that causes a chain of reactions that increases oxidative stress. In the future, when you encounter similar events, the memory is recalled along with the attached emotion. This shapes your perception of things or events that remind you of the original event.

Changing Your Perception

Bruce Lipton talks about rewriting the tape. The tape being the memory that was imprinted during a traumatic event or series of traumatic or stressful events. It is my assertion that its not the memory itself that has to be rewritten but rather the emotion attached to the memory. The emotion stimulates the sympathetic and parasympathetic nervous systems. It is the emotion attached to the memory that causes the trigger. The memory serves as a reminder and a part of the protective system within the brain. If the memory is rewritten then we may also lose the recognition of the warning signs on the road. Let's use the traditional example of primitive human existence, you hear the lion in the jungle while hunting. After your brother gets dragged away by the lion, it creates a traumatic memory in your mind. If that primitive person rewrites the memory of the event, they may not remember the sound of the lion creeping through the jungle nor associate it with danger. However, if they change the fear emotion attached to the memory, then when they go hunting again, they do it with a clear mind, not one overwhelmed with fear. They are also better equipped to recognize the sound of the lion in the

bushes and respond to protect themselves. The same for

you today, change the emotion attached to the memory to

change perception and the negative effects that results

from the bodily changes as a response to the negative or

traumatic event. Keep the memory as a data point of

knowledge. How to change the emotion without

changing the memory? Memory and emotion work

together in a positive feedback loop. Memory, emotion,

and physiological reaction, which leads to the memory,

then the emotions and the physiological response, and so

on. Change any part of the loop and you change the loop.

It's not an instant thing. It takes work. It takes a

conscious change in perception. By seeking a different

understanding of the event and purposely empathizing

with other viewpoints around the event, you begin to

change the emotion attached to the memory of the event.

Thus changing the physiological response to the memory

and turning the pain of the trigger into your power.

NOTES:

Chapter 5

Relationship Between Religion and Health

<u>Control Your Power of Will</u>

"the ability to control your thoughts and actions in order to achieve what you want to do; a strong and determined 'desire to do something that you want to do."[39]

"I AM THAT I AM"

Your spirit is packaged in your will. Before you were born, your will was within you. It is your will to be born that causes you to push through the pain to come into this realm of existence. Your will took part in shaping your personality. Will is a strong and determined desire to do something (or to not do a thing). Some things affecting your will are your beliefs, health, emotions, restfulness, stress level, generational pattern, and perception. To break your spirit, your will must first be

---

[39] will noun - Definition, pictures, pronunciation and usage notes | Oxford Advanced Learner's Dictionary at OxfordLearnersDictionaries.com

broken. Galatians 5:17 says "For the flesh desires what is contrary to the Spirit, and the Spirit what is contrary to the flesh. They are in conflict with each other, so that you are not able to do whatever you want." Your will is more than a want. It is a deep, determined desire. Your spirit represents your creative mind or imagination and your flesh represents your carnal desires. Let's think about this example, you want to live a healthy lifestyle and your favorite thing to do at night is to over-indulge in ice cream before bed. Your wants conflict with one another. Here your spirit wants to eat healthy and your flesh wants to eat ice cream. You can't do whatever you want when this happens. You get/do what you will. Whichever desire is more determined wins. Your will to be healthy or your will to indulge in ice cream. And the factors previously mentioned can either make your will stronger or can kill your will. In this example of healthy living, if you are an emotional eater, at a time of high stress or emotional trauma, your will to eat healthy may be weakened or even broken. However if you witnessed a close family member suffer from diabetes, depending on your perception your determination towards not being sick can increase your will to eat healthy. Keeping your end goal in mind will help strengthen your will to do and be what you imagine for yourself. Not only that but reminding yourself of what achieving your goal means to you will help you maintain control of your will in times of conflict. Remembering your goals and what they mean to you AND making sure it holds weight in your heart is easier said than done. Chances are, you will slip and fall short of your highest self's will. You are human. It is important to be kind to yourself. Not being kind to yourself; not giving yourself grace leads to shame, broken confidence and weakened will. On the contrary, showing yourself grace, kindness, and mercy during and after moments of weakness actually lightens the weight of your emotions and frees up mental space to consider your goals. From that space you spend more time imagining your desired end goals. Repetition makes it more real and it being real to you strengthens your will to manifest it into reality. It shines a bright light on the reality that your goals are achievable. Your imagination then begins to create new ways to achieve your goals. When you get down on yourself, especially after a moment of weakness, the negative emotions cloud your judgment and vision so that instead of relying on your creative mind to work its magic, your lower self is empowered to find paths to escape the self blame and weight of your negative emotions. The result is you making excuses and justifications for your negative actions instead of facing the reality about yourself and your situation so that you can create pathways to freedom from negative patterns to setting new healthy patterns that turn into a new way of being which allows you to make better choices, build self-confidence, and create the life that the Will of your higher self dictates for yourself. What you watch and take in: what you consume with your senses guides your emotions. When it guides you to a negative place, be mindful of all other messages that seep into your consciousness. Messages that lead to negative and past habits. When this happens, you must identify it, see it for what it is, and not let it take control of your power. This is how you take control of your power of Will. There will be times when either you don't recognize the negative messages or triggers, especially after you first create your new image or you recognize them but choose to give into the temptation. Whether or not giving into the temptation is negative or bad, depends on what the temptation is for one, and two, who, what, and how it affects. Going back to our ice cream example, choosing to eat the ice cream is negative because it goes against your health goals.

However it's not a thing to beat yourself up about. Choosing to eat the ice cream knowing you are pre-diabetic or diabetic is negative for you. While it is negative for you and is on your list of personal responsibilities to your higher self's goals, it is at the same time bad for your loved ones because they are hurt by your illness or possible loss of life and takes priority on your list of things to change if you are to achieve your health goal because it is not only a direct antagonist to a goal that can save your life but it also negatively affects your loved ones and only you can control your Will to change. This is a personal responsibility. And you must show yourself grace to be successful and give yourself an honest chance for change. Your choice to act in a way that is emotionally, mentally, or physically harmful to other people, regardless if it goes against your goals, is bad and must take priority. This is a personal responsibility always and a public responsibility depending on what it is. By public I mean anyone outside of yourself and by responsibility I mean, must hold you accountable. This is why societies create court systems, to hold people accountable for doing the most harmful things to others. And the systems must be held accountable by the public in which it serves. What I mean by personal responsibility is that it is your duty to change, and not the public's. Diet is a personal responsibility, for example, and murder or rape is a public responsibility. Some people are assholes. I'm not talking about the slightly jaded, a bit (or even very) cynical, maybe even dark-humored assholes. Because even they show empathy in their "traumatized-by-humans behavior", and "life is dark" kind of way. I'm talking about the antagonistic, "I bully people to make myself feel better", deeply insecure, totally selfish, gaslighty, "I wouldn't know real if it punched me in my face, but I'm gonna scream 'im real' every chance I get" kind of people. You know the narcs, sociopaths, and other bully types of people. Over the centuries more and more of them have been produced on earth. They walk among us and terrorize families, communities, and nations. They will be the downfall of humanity if we allow it. The problem is CONTROL. Those people lack self-control which leads to their deep-rooted sense of insecurity and shame. They will hardly ever admit it because it's too shameful and they will have to become honestly vulnerable which is a weakness to them leading to even more shame. So to make up for this lack of self-control, they seek to control others around them. They make up lies about their world and project that onto others. They use invalidation, gaslighting, triangulation and other bullying tactics like public humiliation to control individuals and even groups of individuals. People who are not lacking in shows of empathy, too often feel bad for these people mistaking their actions as them "just having a bad day". We too often give them passes, sometimes just to avoid their childish temper tantrums. Other times we don't want to deal with their lies and smear campaigns which usually are really just them mirroring their actions and intent onto those of us with audacity enough to stand up to them and not tolerate their antagonistic ways. But when we become passive, when we don't hold these people accountable for their actions, when we just deal with them or smile and agree to not enrage the beast, we are planting seeds for them to reproduce. Their ways spread; in leadership roles, people see that that's how things get done so some adapt the antagonistic ways to move up and advance in their organizations, to earn more money and even to earn more respect and control in family and community systems with antagonistic leaders. In a study that was conducted by Dr. Robert Sapolsky, an American neuroscientist, he accidentally discovered a change in the hierarchy of primates when all the dominant males in the group bullied their way into a trash can of tuberculosis-infected food and died. Dr. Sapolsky was studying their behaviors when he returned to the camp and discovered the horrific accident. He thought his experiment had come to an end with about half of his test subjects dead. Then he observed something unexpected. The less antagonistic primates took dominant roles in the tribe. They lived peacefully. They groomed each other. No one randomly got hit or knocked around by another of them. They shared food. All opposite of their lives with the antagonistic primates who bullied everyone. His research continued and he later discovered that when new young males came into the camp, the more dominant, empathetic primates kept the new young aggressive males in check. I'm not

suggesting that we poison all bullies to death. But there

is something very important we can learn from this study

and other studies on fellow primates. Will is not free but

it comes at a cost. Our Will; our choices; what we want

and decide at any given moment is determined by

biology and society and the two are intertwined from the

roots on up. Human's genetic code is the program we

are born with. Based on it is how we function in the

world. "We" make up society. Society functions based on

the people who make it up. Our genetic code changes

over the course of our life based on societal effects. It's

a closed-looped cycle. The cost of our Will is the energy

we expend to change how we function both on an

individual level then as a society. Change in biology is

the result. And if we do this right and with the right

intentions, we will have a world of leaders who are more

empathetic and less tyrannius. More compassionate

and less power hungry. Stronger and less greedy and

dominating.

NOTES:

Chapter 6

The Limniscate

"Human behavior flows from three main sources: desire,

emotion, and knowledge." - Plato

Most people are born good and remain good people throughout their lives. Some become hardened by life's issues but are still good people at the core. By good I mean empathetic, kind-hearted, do no harm type of people. No matter how cynical or jack-assed they may be. I'm sure most of us have come across that person. There are few people who are born with the inability to feel empathy; the psychopaths of the world who make up about 1% of the global population. At some point (probably in childhood) some of those people who were born "good" joined the ranks of the psychopaths in the cluster B personality group. The cluster B personality group includes, besides psychopaths, people with narcissistic, borderline, histrionic, and antisocial personalities. It's difficult to know exactly what leads a person to develop any of these personalities. Though genetic and environmental factors are two primary causes. The MAOA gene is responsible for regulating levels of serotonin, dopamine and norepinephrine. Serotonin influences happiness, sexual behavior, sleep and other body functions. Dopamine plays a part in memory, motivation, pleasure, and satisfaction. Norepinephrine is important for cognitive function, regulation of arousal, attention, and stress reaction. Studies have linked mutations in the MAOA gene to cluster B personality types.[40,41] MAOA mutations are inherited on the X chromosome. The mutation in the gene expression is on one X chromosome and if a

[40] https://pubmed.ncbi.nlm.nih.gov/10904119/

[41] https://sciencedirect.com/article/abs/pii/S0165178110005342

healthy MAOA is on the other X chromosome in females, it counters the mutated gene. However in males there is only one X chromosome. So if his MAOA gene is mutated there is no other X chromosome to counter it. This is why disorders linked to the X chromosome are more likely to occur in males than females since double mutation is unlikely in both X chromosomes in females.[42] Even though this mutation can be passed onto offspring, it's expression is heavily influenced by environmental factors like childhood maltreatment, complex social traumas, toxins in the air, soil, water and products like food packaging that contains PFAS (per- and poly-fluoro-alkyl substances, a group of

---

[42] https://medlineplus.gov/genetics/condition/monoamine-oxidase-a-deficiency/#inheritance

human-made chemicals that have been used in many

industrial and consumer products since the 1940's)[43,44,]

[45] PFAS and natural toxins like battery acid, fossil fuels,

and burning treated wood which releases harmful

chemicals into the air like arsenic, nitrogen oxide, sulfur

dioxide, and volatile organic chemicals pollute the air,

land and water killing animals, humans, plants, and

insects. They also cause diseases and disorders in

humans and animals, and mutations in plants like more

---

[43]https://www.nature.com/articles/s41598-019-39103-7#:~:text=Aggression%20is%20a%20ubiquitous%20phenomenon,nmodels7%2C8%2C9.

44

https://www.sciencedirect.com/science/article/abs/pii/S0191886912004047

[45]https://www.niehs.nih.gov/health/topics/agents/pfc#:~:text=Per%2Dand%20polyfluoroalkyl%20substances%20(pfas,degrade%20easily%20in%20the%20environment.

aggressive pollen that leads to more severe allergies and other negative health effects in humans.[46,47,48,49,50,51]

Ok, so, these toxins are mostly man-made like PFAS or human controlled like treating wood with arsenic then burning it and releasing poison into the atmosphere. It

---

[46] https://www.cuttingedgefirewood.com/blogs/blog/can-i-burn-pressure-treated-wood#:~:text=Burning%20CCA%20wood%20means%20that,hazardous%20insecticide%20and%20fungi%20chemicals.

[47] https://www.who.int/news-room/fact-sheets/detail/natural-toxins-in-food#:~:text=Some%20natural%20toxins%20can%20be,to%20both%20humans%20and%20livestock.

[48] https://www.who.int/news-room/fact-sheets/detail/pesticide-residues-in-food#:~:text=Pesticides%20are%20potentially%20toxic%20to%20humans%20and,ways%20in%20which%20a%20person%20is%20exposed.&text=When%20people%20come%20into%20contact%20with%20large,include%20cancer%20and%20adverse%20effects%20on%20reproduction.

[49] https://www.ncbi.nlm.nih.gov/pmc/articles/PMC4214967/

[50] https://www.ncbi.nlm.nih.gov/pmc/articles/PMC1461763/

[51] https://yaleclimateconnections.org/2024/05/allergy-symptoms-got-you-down-blame-pollen-and-air-pollution/#:~:text=When%20researchers%20in%20Spain%20compared,be%20false%2C%E2%80%9D%20Fuertes%20says.

has been known that these chemicals and practices have horrible adverse effects on humans and other parts of nature but the activity persists. Large corporations make lots of money of these practices that include known toxic chemicals and despite losing large class action lawsuits, paying out millions of dollars, and seeing first hand the deaths, cancers, child deaths and other suffering they cause to people, the people responsible for making decisions in these companies still choose to value the billions and sometimes trillions of dollars their companies make each year over human lives which are priceless. They even sacrifice their own children's lives for money and power because these toxins are not only in just about everything we use from food packaging to bottled water to soaps and cleaning products to clothing, bedding and other fabrics, and even household furniture and building materials, but they also pollute the atmosphere and are the causes of human influenced global warming which effects every living breathing thing on this planet including the families of these large corporations and contributors of the toxic society. pesticides, hormones, man-made forever chemicals all lead to genetic mutations that change our DNA expression. These changes in DNA expression affect how we experience and interact with the world. For about 2-8% of the population this means developing antagonistic personalities. Unfortunately the confident, ambitious, and manipulative nature of people with these personality types often lead them to positions of leadership. Whether in family structures, organizations, work places, or communities, their toxic traits and behaviors cause trauma and negative stress to people existing and interacting with them. This type of prolonged stress leads to more adverse health effects in the long and short term. It's a vicious cycle. Antagonistic people and cluster B personality types have always been around. In studies conducted with primates, scientists' observations of hierarchical social structures taught that submissive and less dominant primates mimic the behaviors of the more dominant primates in the social group. When an aggressive male or female in the group walks up and knocks a less dominant one down, that less dominant one often goes off and is violent with a primate less dominant then they are. Like how abused, neglected children who get beat on at home, sometimes go to school and bully other children that are less aggressive than them. Or how a mean boss rips into a worker at a staff meeting. Then later that day, the worker who is now having a bad day, yells at their secretary. Some people however, possess gene expressions that cause them to remain empathetic, altruistic, and kind no matter the abuse they experience. In the primate study done by Dr. Sapolsky, once the antagonistic primates were gone, the more dominant non antagonistic members maintained a more pleasant culture in the tribe, running off any newcomers who did not subscribe to their new non-abusive way of living. Most times people just don't want to deal with the situations that antagonism creates, so they give into the bully. It can feel like too much, so people will just agree, smile, and go along, ignoring or avoiding to keep the peace. This kind of reaction rewards the bully and pacifies the demon within these personality types. A Lot of people are just fooled by the cluster B types into thinking it's just them. A person might be gas lit into thinking they are doing something wrong. This is because of cluster B's confidence in their own manipulation tactics. So it isn't seen as manipulation but instead starts to change their own behaviors to accommodate the cluster B personality type. Especially, but not exclusively in the business world. It is like one has to become a narcissist in order to succeed in the business world. And business/work is how people "earn a living". If you don't work, you can't eat, be clothed, live in a good temperature home, ect. Even if you practice horticulture and keep your own garden, you have to participate in commerce to pay rent, mortgage, taxes, buy clothes, ect. And with the rising cost of living, more and more money resources are needed just to survive and most people want to thrive not merely survive. So that means developing tactics and skills to make more sales and drive business. Effective sales and marketing is a whole psychological mind-fuck. The whole goal is really to capture people's attention (whether consciously or subconsciously) and hypnotize them into wanting what you are selling. Effective marketing teaches you to use voice tones & rhythms, que words & phrases, body language & postures, and repetition to mesmerize people. This is because it works when implemented correctly. A business owner, sales person, or marketer is able to increase sales and beat out the competition. Not only does it feed the reward sensors in the brain but it allows the most successful to live lives they once dreamed about and lives that some others can only imagine. It allows them the money resources to go where they want and do what they want and have what they want in a material world. And guess who seems to be best at this type of mesmerizing, hypnotic, psychological mind-fucking. Yup, those with narcissistic and other cluster B personality types. Imagine life as a spiraled, 3D puzzle with the baseline being the middle section. The spiral goes around and outward from baseline in both directions and connects right back at the middle like a lemniscate or infinity symbol.

Both sides of the baseline have positive and negative qualities with one direction from baseline being varying degrees of empathetic and the other direction being varying degrees of antagonistic. Now imagine the forward and backwards "S"shapes of the lemniscate. The forward "S" being humble and the backwards "S" being noble. Ok. Stay with me. This is important. (that's marketing talk for "this is a difficult idea to convey but I need you to really get this because it is important to understand the whole idea"). Ok. There is no real direction in space or in eternity but for illustration purposes and for POV understanding the baseline is where we are born and also where humanity came into existence. Below the baseline is an antagonistic energy at its most distant point, completely void of empathy and varying degrees of antagonism on both sides in descending order up to the baseline. At the baseline is neither empathy or antagonism. Then in ascending order from baseline to the highest point upward of the baseline being the most empathetic. Now both sides to each antagonistic and empathetic have its negative and positive. Now the lemniscate is not a flat 2D shape. It has many dimensions. Infinite even. We exist in 3D + time & space = 4D + consciousness = 5D. The lemniscate has mass. The mass accounts for the shape and has the ability to change the shape of each direction and side of baseline. The line that outlines the shape of the lemniscate is Time itself. Ok. I have faith that I did an effective job at outlining the picture of this idea. Now to color it in. I'm going to tackle this from different angles. So please be patient with the repetition of this. Let's start with the direction of empathy. Going up the positive side from baseline is nobility. This idea of nobility is the idea and act of standing up for what is "right". What is right on this side of the baseline is love for others, self, nature and the value of life over money and possessions. It starts with an internal sense of "do no harm" and goes up to "taking a stand against bad, hurtful actions towards others". It's not completely void of antagonistic traits but the balance tilts in favor of empathy more and more the closer you get to the top being total empathy. now , continue to travel along that part of the lemniscate. You go from the positive side of empathy to the negative side of empathy; being humble. Humbleness is the opposite of nobility. It is holding your head low, not speaking up for what's right or good but also not intentionally aiding in the antagonistic acts. On the negative side of empathy there is humility and sometimes a shame that's felt for being a good person and not standing up for what is right and against what's wrong. Ok, let's keep traveling along this line past the baseline. You will find yourself on the negative side of antagonism. It is important to note that below baseline is a mirrored image of what is above the baseline. Antagonism and empathy mirror each other so that positive and negative are opposite. The positive humble side of the antagonistic direction is backwards to the negative humble side of empathy. On the antagonistic direction from baseline it's more and more humbled, more and more complacent, increasingly supportive of antagonistic behaviors all the way down to totally antagonistic personality types at the lowest point below baseline. Continuing up the other side is the positive side of antagonistic energy which is nobility. This side and direction is filled with boastful destructive energy. Totally selfish, not caring how their actions impact others, not even those closest to them. Keep in mind there are varying degrees and the scale slides based on how far away from baseline and baseline is void of both empathy and antagonism, nobility and humbleness. Baseline is single pointedness, nirvana. Totally naked like a newborn baby. Blank slate. "Nothingness" of existence itself. Full of potential. "To Be" or "I Am" before anything is added. Ok, so for empathy, humbleness is being meek, doing your work, staying in your lane, eyes on the road and going straight in the direction the road leads you. On one hand it's good. It's not being a troublemaker. It's radiating love in a less active way. Overall it's good because empathy and love is good. At the same time it's bad or becomes bad in a world where antagonism has more mass because it means staying quiet about the wrong in the world even though you don't agree. It's in the positive direction of empathy and maybe a higher chance of raising empathetic children in the world who are more noble. What is negative to empathy is positive to antagonism. If you fold the lemniscate in half at the baseline you will see that the negative humble empathy side is directly shadowed by the positive noble antagonistic side and that is exactly how opposites attract. The more boastful antagonist is often found attracted to the humble empath.

Probably mostly because the humble empath doesn't take a stand even though they don't agree. They may not act "bad" but the boastful antagonist can use them as a cover or mask because of their complacency. Humble empaths are often workers and sometimes leaders within companies and organizations led by antagonistic personalities with narcissistic, sociopathic and even psychopathic purposes. But the purpose is masked with the humbled empathic light so that people are drawn in. It's a form of the antagonist's ability to mesmerize. Opposite of that is the noble empath and humble antagonist.Ok this can be a bit tricky and where the mind fuckary of the noble antagonist plays too. The noble empath is the positive side of the empathic direction because they take an active stance against the opposite direction. They switch lanes as needed and use their light as a lamp and sword against darkness. Their eyesight is wide and they are willing and ready to make "good trouble", not being complacent with antagonistic energy. They stand up for and defend what is right and good in the world. Also being selfless like the humble empath. The noble empath has traditionally been pointed or highlighted as the martyr, usually by the antagonistic personalities to discourage this type of boldness but the antagonistic energies encourage the humble empathy instead because the noble empaths are much less easy to be used and manipulated. Again folding at the baseline, the noble empath is shadowed by the humble antagonist. The humble antagonistic energy is more of the wolf in sheep's clothing.

It's the antagonistic side that will play the victim of the noble empath in public to help prove the noble antagonist's point of manipulation that the noble empath is really the bad or negative one. The mirror. The humble antagonist shadows the noble empath casting a shade on the good works of the noble empath. Tricking people closest to baseline to attack and go against the noble empath along with any high empathic humble energy that refuses to support the antagonist. I won't give examples of these four personality types or energies though I'm sure some come to mind while you are reading this. Both famous figures and those in your life. My goal is to paint the picture of a new side of reality so that collectively we can bring that into reality.

Now, we have pulled the veil back of the below baseline antagonists to see the full lemniscate picture. The current and maybe forever reality is that humanity, as one energy, travels along and settles on different points of the lemniscate at different speeds at different times in human existence. Remember, the lemniscate has mass and the total mass is the total weight of human energy on the planet or in existence. The shape of the lemniscate shifts based on weight distribution. Right now it seems that more and more people are falling below baseline. Antagonistic energy has been ruling the world, tilting the shape downwards in favor of the antagonistic energy causing the mass of people to sink to the bottom of the lemniscate like sand in an hourglass made of elastic, stretching the lines of time in the antagonist's favor.

The mass gives weight to each side, the side with the

most weight is the side the shape of existence stands on.

The mass also stretches the lines of time, creating a

shorter or longer time-line on either side of the baseline.

The battle is to stretch the timeline, increase the mass

and tip existence to stand in the favor of love and

empathy for as long as possible, if not for eternity.

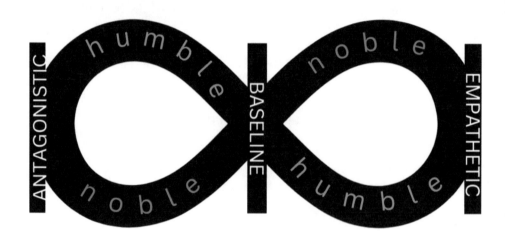

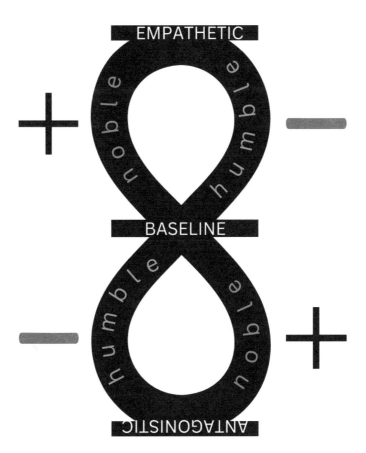

NOTES:

NOTES:

NOTES:

NOTES:

Made in the USA
Columbia, SC
06 December 2024

48630888R00067